# CONTENTS

Venus and Serena Williams have faced each other on the court numerous times in singles finals. They have also teamed up to win a record number of doubles titles, too.

Few tennis players have changed the world of tennis quite like Venus and Serena Williams. Between them, they have won most of the sport's biggest tournaments—individually and as a doubles team—record amounts of prize money, and a total of five Olympic gold medals. In the early 2000s, the tennis star sisters dominated the sport's Grand Slam events, the four most important tennis tournaments.

The sisters grew up in a poor area of Los Angeles. As youngsters, they had to fight against racist attitudes to succeed. Through talent and hard work, they became two of the most successful women's tennis players of all time.

The sisters have used their fame to fight for equal pay for women tennis players and raise money for charity. For women today, there are few better role models than Venus and Serena, two truly great athletes who have made a real difference in their communities.

# CHAPTER 1

# THE WILLIAMS SISTERS' STORY

Richard Williams always wanted his daughters, Venus (born June 17, 1980, in Lynwood, California) and Serena (born September 26, 1981, in Saginaw, Michigan), to have a better life than he had. In the poor, crime-ridden neighborhood of Compton, California, where the Williams' lived, there were few opportunities for young African Americans to better themselves.

After watching a tennis match on television, Richard Williams decided he would coach his daughters in tennis, with the aim of setting them on the path of great sporting careers.

Serena Williams has come a long way since she learned to play tennis on the public courts in Compton. Here, she is seen in action at the 2013 Australian Open in Melbourne, Australia.

It was a bold plan, not least because tennis in the United States at the time was dominated by white players from more privileged backgrounds.

When Venus was just five and Serena was four, their father took them to the public tennis courts in Compton for the first time. From that moment on, tennis became their life.

It was not easy for the Williams sisters to enter the world of junior tennis. They often had to put up with racist comments from the parents of other players, who resented their success and ability. Yet, it only made Venus and Serena more determined to succeed.

## STAR STATS

As junior tennis players, both Venus and Serena achieved amazing records. Venus won every one of her 63 matches. Serena won all but three of her 49 matches.

# TEENAGE STARS

It was a mark of the Williams sisters' abilities that they did not wait until the age of 16 to turn professional, which is when most tennis players turn pro. Both were just 14 when they played their first professional matches.

Success wasn't instant for the Williams sisters, but when it came few were surprised.

Serena on the court at the 1999 TIG Tennis Classic. By then, there were few tennis rivals who could respond to either of the sisters' big serves and powerful shots.

The sisters had long been thought of as future greats. At the age of 17, Venus reached the final of the 1997 U.S. Open. Two years later, Serena won the U.S. Open, her first Grand Slam success.

By the time Serena was crowned U.S. Open champion in 1999, the Williams sisters were a dominant force in women's tennis. Together, they won doubles titles at the French Open and U.S. Open.

In July 2000, Venus won her first grand slam tournament, at Wimbledon. The era of Venus and Serena Williams's domination of women's tennis had begun.

## STAR STATS

Between 1998 and 2002, Venus Williams won 21 consecutive matches at the Miami Masters tournament, a record equaled only by all-time great Steffi Graf.

# TOTAL DOMINATION

By the early 2000s, the Williams sisters were simply unstoppable. Close off the court, they became huge rivals on it as they battled to win titles, especially the four Grand Slams every year.

Time and time again, Venus and Serena found themselves playing each other in the finals of major tournaments, with father Richard looking on from the stands.

Venus and Serena first faced each other in a Grand Slam final at the U.S. Open in 2001. In tennis, matches are made up of games and sets.

## STAR STATS

In January 2003, Serena won the Australian Open. By doing so, she became the fifth female tennis player in history to hold all four Grand Slam titles at the same time.

As of July 2013, Venus Williams has won 7 Grand Slam singles titles, with her younger sister winning an amazing 16. Only three female players, Martina Navratilova, Steffi Graf, and Chris Evert, have won more.

A player must win at least six games to win a set, and women players must win at least two sets—the best of three—to win the match. On this occasion, Venus retained her title by beating Serena two sets to nil.

A year later, the situation reversed when Serena defeated Venus for her first French Open title, and then went on to beat her sister at both Wimbledon and the U.S. Open.

# DOUBLING UP

It's not just in singles tennis matches that the Williams sisters stand out. Unlike many other top singles tennis stars, they're also huge fans of playing doubles.

Venus and Serena Williams have played doubles together from an early age. In fact, they've formed the most formidable doubles team in the history of women's tennis. Since winning the women's doubles competition at the French Open in 1999, they have remained unbeaten in Grand Slam doubles finals. To date, they've won an astonishing 13 titles. Together, they've won five Wimbledon finals, four Australian Open finals, two French Open titles, and two U.S. Open titles.

Perhaps the most prestigious doubles titles the sisters have won are those while representing the United States at the Olympic Games. They first won gold together at the Sydney, Australia, games in 2000, repeated the feat in Beijing, China, in 2008, and won gold again at London in 2012.

The Williams sisters proudly display their trophy after winning the U.S. Open women's doubles title in 2009.

# MORE THAN TENNIS

Through the mid-2000s, both Venus and Serena endured spells on the sidelines due to injuries and personal problems. As their careers progressed, the Williams sisters devoted less time to tennis and more time to other activities.

Although they rarely miss Grand Slam tournaments—particularly their favorites, the U.S. Open and Wimbledon—they are not regularly seen at smaller tour events. This has brought them into conflict with the Women's Tennis Association (WTA) and television commentators. The WTA and commentators argue that Venus and Serena are the biggest names in women's tennis, so therefore they harm the sport when they take time out from playing.

Having played tennis since they were young, however, it's perhaps unsurprising that the sisters have begun to pursue other interests. They have increasingly devoted more time to running their own businesses and contributing to communities through charity work.

Venus and Serena Williams (above) are still regulars at the world's Grand Slam events. Without fail, the sisters draw huge crowds of people who come to see the tennis legends in action.

## STAR STATS

Having won nearly $50 million in prize money, Serena Williams is the highest-earning female tennis player ever.

15

# CHAPTER 2

# SERVING UP CHANGE

Throughout their lives, Venus and Serena have sought to bring about change. They changed their own lives by working hard to become world class tennis players.

Off the tennis court, the sisters are also committed to change. Whether this is by campaigning for equal pay for sportswomen, successfully running their own businesses,

As black women in a sport dominated by white players, Venus (below) and Serena Williams have proven that anyone can succeed if they work hard and make the most of their talent.

or even becoming the first black women to become part-owners of a National Football League (NFL) franchise (they bought a stake in the Miami Dolphins in 2009), Venus and Serena have consistently challenged gender inequality.

Since their very earliest days as teenage players, they've also been hugely committed to using tennis as a vehicle for change. In 1995, Venus won an award for teaching tennis to kids in inner-city areas. Ever since, the sisters have tried to use their talent and fame to raise money for charity and improve the lives of those less fortunate than themselves.

## STAR STATS

In February 2002, Venus became the first black woman to top the world tennis rankings. In that same year, Venus and Serena became the first sisters to be ranked Nos. 1 and 2 in the world.

# INNER-CITY LIFE

Tennis helped Venus and Serena Williams to make better lives for themselves. This taught them a valuable lesson. If excelling at tennis lifted them out of poverty, it could do the same for other disadvantaged American children.

In 2011, both Venus (below, second from left) and Serena took part in coaching clinics around the United States as part of the World Team Tennis league tour. Both sisters played for the league's Washington Kastles.

Throughout their careers, Venus and Serena Williams have inspired countless disadvantaged children and young people by holding tennis coaching clinics on public courts and in schools.

Sometimes, these coaching sessions take place around major tennis tournaments, such as the Miami Masters, Wimbledon, or the U.S. Open. At other times, they're put on by charities that the sisters support. Venus and Serena have also visited countless schools, clubs, and tennis academies to teach kids there the secrets behind their astonishing success.

## STAR STATS

At the U.S. Open in 2007, Venus set a new world record for the fastest recorded serve by a woman in a main-draw (ranked player) match, 129 miles per hour (207.6 km/h).

# PLAYING FOR CHARITY

From 2004 to 2007, Venus and Serena used their on-court rivalry to entertain fans and raise money for charity. Each year they took a month out of their schedule to take part in the McDonald's Williams Sisters Tour, a series of exhibition matches that raised money for the Ronald McDonald House charity and other local charities.

The McDonald's Williams Sisters Tour was hugely successful. Every year, the tour visited three different cities, with Venus and Serena playing to crowds of up to 10,000 people.

## STAR STATS

In June 2010, Serena Williams became the first professional women's tennis player to win the Australian Open five times.

In 2004, Venus and Serena teamed up with former Olympic champion sprinter Carl Lewis to launch the McDonald's World Children's Day kickoff event in Los Angeles.

The tour raised thousands of dollars for charity.

Talking about the tour in 2005, Venus said, "This is one of the best things we've done together... because it benefits so many charities... It makes us proud to be a part of something that's much bigger and much more important than what we do as tennis players..."

As part of the tour, Venus and Serena visited local charities in each of the cities they traveled to, and also held tennis coaching clinics for disadvantaged children in the cities.

# HELPING HANDS FOR HAITI

Both Venus and Serena have played a key part in pulling the tennis community together to help the victims of natural disasters.

In January 2010, Serena joined forces with top men's tennis star Roger Federer. They organized a charity event to raise money for victims of the 2010 Haiti earthquake, which killed 220,000 people and left almost 3 million people homeless.

The "Hit for Haiti" event featured short matches between the world's top players, and was played the day before the Australian Open. Roger and Serena worked tirelessly to involve other top tennis players.

The charity event was a huge success and raised more than $185,000 toward the Haiti Earthquake Disaster Relief Fund. Ever since, the Australian Open has held a charity event, called "Rally for Relief," the day before the tournament itself begins.

Serena Williams and Roger Federer played together in a mixed doubles match during the Hit for Haiti event on January 17, 2010, in Melbourne, Australia.

# AFRICAN DREAM

It's not just women and girls in the United States that Venus and Serena Williams hope to inspire. In the fall of 2012, they traveled to Africa to tour Nigeria and South Africa for a charity called Breaking the Mould.

The idea was simple. The two most famous black sportswomen of all time would travel to Africa, hold coaching clinics, play some exhibition matches, and talk to girls and young women about their achievements. Venus and Serena hoped to encourage "more women to break molds that have stood between them and their potential," according to a press release about the charity.

The trip was a huge success. Fans gathered to see Venus and Serena wherever they went, and local children were thrilled to meet two of their sporting heroines.

"We're here to empower young girls and let them know that if you dare to dream, you can achieve any goal you want to," Serena told reporters in Lagos, a city in Nigeria. "We were able to break the mold when tennis was very dominated by white

Venus (right) and Serena (left) joined a girls' dance troop during a program called "Kick Like a Girl" as part of their visit to Nigeria to inspire girls and women.

people. To have a face of color come in and dominate showed it doesn't matter what your background is and where you come from, if you have dreams and goals, that's all that matters."

# CHAPTER 3

# CHANGING CHILDREN'S LIVES

Venus and Serena Williams have never forgotten their roots. They may now both be multimillionaires, but there was a time in their past when their parents were poor. Tennis gave the sisters the opportunity to change their lives, and ever since they've been committed to helping children from similar backgrounds do the same.

From the moment they became professional tennis players in the 1990s, the Williams sisters have devoted a lot of time and money to helping children's charities.

The sisters' fame on-court has helped them raise millions for many different charitable causes.

Whether visiting sick children in the hospital, helping set up schools in Africa, or creating charities, giving children a head start in life has long been a priority for the sisters.

Since the mid-2000s, both Venus and Serena have been involved with a California-based charity called the OWL Foundation, which was started by their mother. The foundation funds programs that offer teenagers who have struggled in school the chance to learn new skills. This is just one example of the sisters' commitment to helping young people improve their lives.

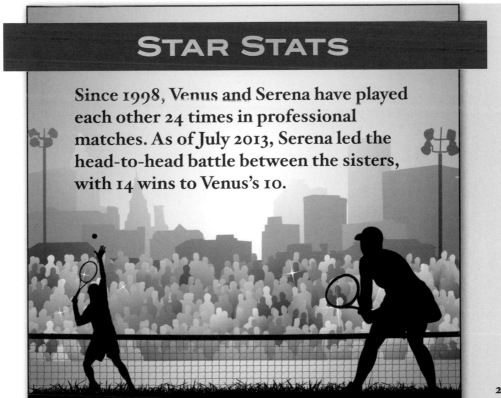

## STAR STATS

Since 1998, Venus and Serena have played each other 24 times in professional matches. As of July 2013, Serena led the head-to-head battle between the sisters, with 14 wins to Venus's 10.

27

# THE SERENA WILLIAMS SECONDARY SCHOOL

Throughout her years of charity work, Serena's focus has remained strongly on education. The tennis star constantly highlights how achieving at school and college can positively change the lives of young people around the world.

Serena Williams received a warm welcome when she spoke at the opening of the Serena Williams Secondary School in Matooni, Kenya, in November 2008.

In 2008, Serena joined forces with a U.S. charity called Build African Schools. The charity, which counts legendary South African leader Nelson Mandela among its founders, raises money to pay for the building of new schools in Africa. Serena was inspired by the charity's aim to allow more poor African children to attend school, and decided to donate a large amount of money to the charity.

In November 2008, the Serena Williams Secondary School opened in Makueni District, near Nairobi in Kenya. Serena attended the opening of the school, alongside almost 10,000 children and 8,000 adults, who had come to see one of the world's most famous sportswomen.

Since then, Serena has opened another school in Kenya, 18 miles (29 km) away from the first. Both schools are equipped with computers, books, and connection to the Internet, all rare in that part of Africa. Through Serena's backing, hundreds of Kenyan children have been able to go to school.

# THE SERENA WILLIAMS FOUNDATION

In 2008, Serena Williams traveled to Africa to attend the opening of a new school her generous donations had helped build. When she returned to the United States, she decided to set up her own charity.

In 2009, she launched the Serena Williams Foundation, which works to better the lives of the children of victims of violent crime throughout the United States. The charity's work honors her and Venus's half-sister, Yetunde, who was shot dead in 2003.

## STAR STATS

In 2009, Serena Williams became the first women's tennis player to win more than $6 million in prize money in one season.

The foundation also aims to help young people who wish to study at college but do not have the financial means to do so.

One of the Serena Williams Foundation's first successes was a project called the "92K Mission," which raised $92,000 for charity in under 92 days. Serena started the project after the International Tennis Federation refused to donate to charity any of the $92,000 she was fined for bad behavior during the U.S. Open.

Serena works with a student at a school she helped build in Africa. She and Venus donate not just money, but their time to worthy causes.

# SPREADING GOODWILL

For many years, Venus and Serena have been spokeswomen for UNICEF, a worldwide charity run by the United Nations. UNICEF works to better the lives of poor children all over the world.

Every year, UNICEF appoints Goodwill Ambassadors. These are people, usually high-profile celebrities, who travel around the world visiting charity projects, talking to reporters, and suggesting solutions to problems.

## STAR STATS

At the 2000 Olympic Games in Sydney, Venus Williams became the second woman to win gold medals in both the singles and doubles competitions at the same Games. In 2012, Serena became the third woman to achieve this at the Olympic Games in London.

The UNICEF Schools for Africa program helps schools such as this one in Malawi, which received 420 desks for its pupils.

Serena first volunteered with UNICEF in 2006, when she traveled to Ghana, in Africa, to assist a health campaign. There, she helped a team of volunteer health workers give children injections to protect them from deadly diseases.

In 2011, Serena was appointed one of UNICEF's Goodwill Ambassadors, a role she used to promote the charity's Schools for Africa and Schools for Asia programs.

# CHAPTER 4

# CHANGING THE GAME

What makes an inspirational athlete? Is it their success on the field, court, or track? Or is it their community and charity work, and how they live their lives? In all of these cases, Venus and Serena Williams are inspirational figures.

The sisters are great role models to young women. They are talented, successful, and use their fame and fortune for charity. They champion equal rights for women, and do their best to inspire young women to follow their example.

As a doubles team, Venus and Serena are formidable. Their legendary partnership sets a great example to upcoming young tennis stars.

In the history of tennis, the sisters are unique. When they first began playing the game, Venus and Serena had to overcome racism from the parents of their opponents. It was unheard of for two black girls from Compton to play tennis, let alone become Grand Slam champions.

Venus and Serena have spent 20 years changing the game of tennis, and most likely will continue to do so for the rest of their lives. They are truly inspirational women.

## STAR STATS

Venus and Serena have dominated the annual WTA Awards. In the last decade, Serena has won the prized "Player of the Year" award four times, and Venus once.

# Fighting for Fair Pay for Women

Until Venus and Serena entered the world of tennis, female tennis players were compared unfavorably to male players, and never seen as equals. Although the women's game had produced some superb athletes, they were paid less than their male counterparts.

The Williams sisters believed this was unfair—not because they wanted to earn more money, but because they thought that female players should be paid the same as males.

They decided to launch a campaign to force the French Open and Wimbledon, the two oldest Grand Slam tournaments, to pay women players the same as men. In 2006, Venus wrote an opinion that appeared in the British newspaper *The Times* arguing that Wimbledon organizers were on the "wrong side of history." She ended the piece with, "I intend to keep doing everything I can until Billie Jean King's original dream of equality is made real."

Later the same year, Venus spearheaded an international campaign for equal rights for all sportswomen. By early 2007, the battle was won. Wimbledon and the French Open both announced that in future, men and women would receive the same amount of prize money. It was a victory not just for Venus Williams, but also for sportswomen around the world.

Venus Williams holds the trophy she won at the Barclays Dubai Tennis Championships in 2009. The win marked the 40th singles title of her career.

# IMPRESSIVE ROLE MODELS

Venus and Serena's fight for equal pay for women is an example of their strength of character and their will to succeed in whatever they do. It's a determined attitude that they've transferred to all their other interests off the court, too, especially their businesses.

Venus has been very successful in the world of business. She owns a number of companies, including V Starr Interiors, which provides designs for apartments and office interiors. Her other passion is clothing design. In 2007, she set up her own fashion company, EleVen. Serena, too, has moved into fashion. Since 2009, she has designed a range of accessories for the Home Shopping Network.

In 2009, the sisters bought a stake in the Miami Dolphins football team. It was a historic move in which Serena and Venus became the first ever black women to own part of an NFL franchise.

**Venus models one of her EleVen outfits for women.**

# SELF-HELP STARS

The Williams sisters' unique life stories and experiences have shaped the way they live their lives and view the world around them. They've decided to share these experiences with fans by writing a number of inspirational books.

In 2005, Venus and Serena teamed up with author Hilary Beard to write the self-help book *Serving from the Hip: 10 Rules for Living, Loving, and Winning*. The book detailed the sisters' "10 rules for life," which include developing a positive daily schedule and healthy eating habits, great personal hygiene, and proper money management. Like many of their projects, the book was a huge success.

In 2010, Venus wrote her own self-help book, this time with author Kelly E. Carter. *Come to Win: How Sports Can Help You Top Your Profession* was another huge smash, appearing in the top five entries on the *New York Times* best seller list. The book combined Venus's tennis background and business interests. It featured advice for succeeding in life, business, and sports from company executives, movie stars, and former athletes. Contributors to the book included basketball star Magic Johnson and tennis player Billie Jean King, as well as doctors and even politicians, including former U.S. president Bill Clinton.

Fans gathered in huge numbers at a bookstore in Dallas, Texas, when Venus Williams signed copies of her book *Come to Win*, in July 2010.

# Sports Icons

Throughout their careers, the Williams sisters have challenged convention and critics, from the parents of their junior opponents to tennis authorities and journalists. They've shown that black women from poor backgrounds can succeed not only in sport, but in business, too.

The riches that their success has brought them have provided the sisters with a comfortable life, but have also helped them financially support a number of good causes.

The charities and organizations they support reflect the sisters' belief that anyone can make it, regardless of the color of their skin or background. This is what drives the Serena Williams Foundation, the sisters' work with the OWL Foundation, and their love of giving free coaching clinics on public courts. Long after the Williams sisters have retired from professional tennis, this work will continue, leaving a lasting impression on all involved.

Shown on the court during a doubles match, Venus and Serena Williams remain global stars both on and off the court.

**1994:** At the age of 14, Venus makes her professional tennis debut at the Bank West Classic in Oakland, California.

**1995:** At the age of 14, Serena makes her professional tennis debut at the Bell Challenge tournament in Quebec City, Canada.

**1999:** Venus and Serena win their first Grand Slam doubles titles, at the French Open and the U.S. Open. Serena wins her first grand slam singles title, winning the U.S. Open.

**2000:** Venus wins Wimbledon, the U.S. Open, and the women's singles gold medal at the 2000 Olympic Games. With Serena, she wins the Wimbledon women's doubles title, and the women's doubles gold at the Olympics.

**2003:** Serena beats Venus in the Australian Open final.

**2004:** Venus and Serena raise over $200,000 for charity on the first of four McDonald's Williams Sisters Tours.

**2005:** Venus wins her third Wimbledon title.

**2008:** Venus wins her fifth Wimbledon title, beating Serena in the final. The sisters win their second doubles gold medal at the Beijing Olympics.

**2008:** Serena helps to fund the construction of the Serena Williams Secondary School in Matooni, Kenya.

**2009:** Venus and Serena buy a share in the Miami Dolphins and Serena opens a second school in Kenya.

**2012:** Venus and Serena win their third doubles gold medal at the Olympic Games. Serena also wins the singles gold.

**2013:** Serena regains the WTA No. 1 ranking, which she has held five times before.

**2013:** Wins at Wimbledon and the U.S. Open bring Serena's total of Grand Slam titles to 17.

### Kevin Durant
The National Basketball Association (NBA) and Olympic Team USA basketball star has raised money for various charities, including a $1 million donation to the America Red Cross to help victims of the Oklahoma City tornado in 2013.

### Jeff Gordon
The leading National Association for Stock Car Auto Racing (NASCAR) driver works tirelessly to raise money for cancer charities.

### Robert Griffin III
The pro football player began volunteering for a number of charities while in college.

### Mia Hamm
The leading soccer player's Mia Hamm Foundation raises money for families of children suffering from rare diseases.

### Tony Hawk
The skateboarding legend's charity, The Tony Hawk Foundation, has provided more than $3.4 million to build 400 skate parks around the United States.

### Derek Jeter
The New York Yankees shortstop started his Turn 2 Foundation to support youth programs across the United States.

### Magic Johnson
The NBA legend founded the Magic Johnson Foundation in 1991, to fund a range of educational projects. Today, 250,000 young Americans benefit from its funded projects every year.

### Peyton and Eli Manning
The record-breaking Super Bowl MVP brothers support many causes through fundraising, including the work of the PeyBack Foundation, the charity set up by Peyton Manning.

### Kurt Warner
The former Super Bowl MVP's First Things First Foundation improves the lives of impoverished children.

**community** A group of people in one particular area.

**disadvantaged** To have few opportunities in life.

**dominated** Completely controlled.

**doubles** A tennis match played between two teams of two people.

**equality** The idea that people should be treated the same, regardless of age, skin color, or gender.

**executives** People who hold senior positions in companies.

**formidable** Impressive, a powerful force.

**fundraising** Holding events, or collecting donations, in order to raise money for charity.

**inspirational** Someone who sets a good example and inspires people.

**mixed doubles** A tennis match played between two teams of two people, with each team consisting of one male and one female player.

**natural disasters** Events, such as earthquakes, floods, or volcanic eruptions, that are caused by natural rather than human forces and that destroy life and property.

**potential** The possibility of future greatness.

**poverty** Being poor, with little or no money.

**progressed** Moved forward.

**retired** Having stopped performing a role or a job.

**rivals** Two people who compete against each other.

**role models** People whose good behavior and attitudes inspire others.

**serve** The movement a player makes to deliver the ball to his or her opponent.

**sets** Stages of a tennis match comprised of six games.

**singles** A tennis match between two people.

**spearheaded** Led something.

**tournaments** Competitions that take place in one place over a set period of time.

# BOOKS

Bailey, Diane. *Venus and Serena Williams: Tennis Champions* (Sports Families). New York, NY: Rosen Central, 2010.

Findlay Watson, Galadriel. *Venus and Serena Williams* (Great African American Women). New York, NY: Weigl Publishers Inc, 2005.

Marcovitz, Hal. *Venus and Serena Williams* (Modern Role Models). Broomall, PA: Mason Crest Publishers, 2009.

Roza, Greg. *Venus and Serena Williams: The Sisters of Tennis*. New York, NY: Rosen Publishing Group, 2005.

Williams, Venus and Serena Williams. *How to Play Tennis*. New York, NY: DK Children's Publishing, 2004.

# WEBSITES

Due to the changing nature of Internet links, Rosen Publishing has developed an online list of Websites related to the subject of this book. This site is updated regularly. Please use this link to access the list:

http://www.rosenlinks.com/mad/will

# VENUS & SERENA WILLIAMS

## IN THE COMMUNITY

MATT ANNISS

Britannica®
Educational Publishing

IN ASSOCIATION WITH

ROSEN
EDUCATIONAL SERVICES

Published in 2014 by Britannica Educational Publishing (a trademark of Encyclopædia Britannica, Inc.) in association with The Rosen Publishing Group, Inc.
29 East 21st Street, New York, NY 10010

Distributed exclusively by Rosen Publishing.
To see additional Britannica Educational Publishing titles, go to rosenpublishing.com

First Edition

**Britannica Educational Publishing**
J.E. Luebering: Director, Core Reference Group
Anthony L. Green: Editor, Compton's by Britannica

**Rosen Publishing**
Hope Lourie Killcoyne: Executive Editor
Jeanne Nagle: Senior Editor
Nelson Sá: Art Director

**Library of Congress Cataloging-in-Publication Data**

Anniss, Matt.
Venus & Serena Williams in the community/Matt Anniss.
    pages cm.—(Making a difference: athletes who are changing the world)
Includes bibliographical references and index.
ISBN 978-1-62275-170-9 (library binding)—ISBN 978-1-62275-173-0 (pbk.)—
ISBN 978-1-62275-174-7 (6-pack)
1. Williams, Venus, 1980—Juvenile literature. 2. Williams, Serena, 1981—Juvenile literature. 3. Tennis players—United States—Biography—Juvenile literature. 4. African American women tennis players—Biography—Juvenile literature. I. Title.
GV994.A1A56 2013
796.342092'52—dc23
[B]

2013024609

*Manufactured in the United States of America*